Joseph Towers, John Palmer

A Sermon, Preached at New Broad-Street, August 1, 1779

occasioned by the death of - Caleb Fleming - who departed this life July 21, 1779 in the eighty-first year of his age - with the oration delivered at the interment by Joseph Towers

Joseph Towers, John Palmer

A Sermon, Preached at New Broad-Street, August 1, 1779
occasioned by the death of - Caleb Fleming - who departed this life July 21, 1779 in the eighty-first year of his age - with the oration delivered at the interment by Joseph Towers

ISBN/EAN: 9783337734398

Printed in Europe, USA, Canada, Australia, Japan

Cover: Foto ©Lupo / pixelio.de

More available books at **www.hansebooks.com**

A
SERMON,

PREACHED AT NEW BROAD-STREET,

AUGUST 1, 1779,

OCCASIONED BY THE

DEATH

OF THE LATE

Rev[d]. CALEB FLEMING, D. D.

WHO DEPARTED THIS LIFE JULY 21, 1779,

IN THE EIGHTY-FIRST YEAR OF HIS AGE.

BY JOHN PALMER.

WITH THE

ORATION,

DELIVERED AT THE

INTERMENT,

BY JOSEPH TOWERS.

LONDON:

PRINTED FOR J. JOHNSON, IN ST. PAUL'S CHURCH-YARD; AND C. DILLY, IN THE POULTRY.

M.DCC.LXXIX.

IT is at the requeſt of the affectionate and long happy conſort, but now ſorrowing widow, of my highly eſteemed friend, the late Reverend, and truly venerable, Dr. Caleb Fleming, that I am this day to addreſs you, on his diſmiſſion from this ſcene of labour and trial; after having attained, through the favour of Providence, to the uncommon age of almoſt eighty-one years.

I could not refuſe my beſt endeavours, to perform this laſt public inſtance of reſpect to the memory of one, whoſe character I ſo much revered, and with whom I had the pleaſure of a long and peculiar intimacy. His relatives, and other friends who may be preſent on this occaſion, particularly thoſe, who have enjoyed the benefit of his paſtoral ſervices; to whom his worth muſt be better known than I can deſcribe it, will kindly accept

 the

the attempt, ſhort as it may fall of their convictions and my wiſhes.

The words I have choſen to inſiſt on, becauſe in a high degree characteriſtic of our departed friend, and, at the ſame time, replete with admonition and comfort, are thoſe of the Apoſtle Paul,

2 COR. I. 12.

For our rejoicing is this, the teſtimony of our conſcience, that in ſimplicity and godly ſincerity, not with fleſhly wiſdom, but by the grace of God, we have had our converſation in the world.

ST. Paul, whoſe principle and line of conduct, and whoſe happy experience, conſequent upon his ſteady adherence to them, are deſcribed in the paſſage now read, was by his profeſſion as a Chriſtian, and ſtill more by his office as an apoſtle, expoſed to peculiar difficulties and dangers. Pure and excellent as the religion of Jeſus is in its nature, and mighty as the evi-

dence

dence was, with which it was attended, of its divine original; on its firſt publication, it met with a general and violent oppoſition. Both Jews and Gentiles, widely as they differed in their religious tenets and uſages, conſidered Chriſtianity as a dangerous innovation; and thought themſelves highly concerned, if poſſible, to defeat the ſucceſs of it. Hence the far greater part of both theſe claſſes of men not only rejected it themſelves, but alſo united in their endeavours to diſcourage the profeſſion of it, by the moſt contemptuous and injurious treatment of thoſe who ventured to make it. And as the alteration, which the Chriſtian ſcheme was deſigned to introduce, by ſubſtituting a new and very different inſtitution of religion, inſtead of the former Jewiſh and Heathen eſtabliſhments, could not but be particularly offenſive to thoſe who were in authority; the aid of the ſecular arm was therefore not wanting to ſupport the clamours of the people, and bring the abettors of this new doctrine to what they judged a condign puniſhment. More particularly was the reſentment of an infidel world levelled againſt thoſe, who, while they avowed the Chriſtian faith themſelves, were alſo engaged in bringing over others to the reception of it. Accordingly, when malice had perpetrated, to the utmoſt of its power, its cruel deſigns on the perſon of the great Founder of our holy religion, by putting him to the painful and ignominious death of the croſs; the ſame evil ſpirit continued to exert itſelf in perſecuting the apoſtles of our Lord, who, agreeably to the ſpecial commiſſion which they had received from him, were employed in the communication of that word of truth, which at firſt began to be ſpoken by the Lord Chriſt himſelf. St. Paul was no leſs diſtinguiſhed by his ſufferings in the Chriſtian cauſe, than by the zeal which he manifeſted in the ſupport of it; and the greatneſs of the one, in ſuch a ſtate of things, is, indeed, naturally to be accounted for, by the vigour and ſteadineſs of the other. In the epiſtles of this apoſtle, we have frequent mention of the troubles he underwent, or to which he ſtood expoſed; though never in any ſuch way as was inconſiſtent with true fortitude of mind, or, indeed, in any other, but what was clearly and ſtrongly expreſſive of it. In the chapter where our text is, he particularly addreſſes the Corinthian converts on this ſubject; acknowledging, in terms of the warmeſt gratitude, the abundant ſupport with which he was favoured by the God of all comfort; and this with the benevolent deſign of ſtrengthening the minds of the perſons, to whom he wrote; who, as profeſſors of the ſame religion, though only in a private capacity, were partakers with him in ſuffering on that account. He ſpeaks of one deliverance, which he had experienced, when in imminent danger of death, which animated his confidence in the ſame divine power and mercy, to which he thankfully aſcribes this eſcape, for his further preſervation, as long as Infinite Wiſdom ſaw fit. He was, however, prepared for the worſt; being fully determined, that, with the divine aid, he would ſtill continue faithfully to diſcharge the important duties of his apoſtolic office; whatever perils might await him in the execution of it: and under all his paſt trials, and thoſe to which he was further liable, there was one grand ſource of conſolation, from which he derived the firmeſt ſupport to his faith and hope; and what that was, he informs us in the text; *for our rejoicing is this, the teſtimony of our conſcience, that in ſimplicity, and godly ſincerity, not with fleſhly wiſdom, but by the grace of God, we have had our converſation in the world.* It may not be altogether undeſerving of notice, that, though it is to be ſuppoſed St. Paul had a more direct reference to himſelf in this deſcription; he yet makes uſe of plural terms, including other of his fellow-labourers in the gospel, and hereby suggesting, with a generosity of heart, worthy of imitation, that he considered them, not only as professedly embarked with him in one noble design, but also as conducting themselves on the same excellent principle, and pursuing equally upright measures, for the accomplishment of it. And there is the more reason for supposing this to have been his view; as, in the first verse of the chapter, he speaks of Timothy, whom he calls our brother, as being with him, at the time when he wrote this epistle.

The words are in themselves so plain, as to need but little comment upon them. They represent, in a clear and forcible manner, what that spirit, or disposition of mind, was, which actuated and governed him in all his services, as an apostle of Christ, and the whole of his behaviour, towards all, with whom he had any connection, or to whom, under the guidance of divine Providence, he was led to miniſter. This was, ſimplicity, or plainneſs of heart, and ſincerity before God, or a ſincere, prevailing regard to his approbation and acceptance—not a fleſhly wiſdom, that is, not that worldly policy, which ſeeketh its own private emolument or ſecular gain—but, on the contrary, the ſpirit of that wiſdom which is from above, whoſe illuminating and animating influences were graciouſly imparted to him in an eminent degree. Such was the complexion and happy turn of the apoſtle's mind; theſe the principles on which he acted.

If any further illuſtration were neceſſary; the apoſtle has himſelf given us a ſufficient one in the ivth Chapter of this Epiſtle, Ver. 2. where he ſays—*We have renounced the hidden things of diſhoneſty, not walking in craftineſs, nor handling the word of God deceitfully, but by manifeſtation of the truth, commending ourſelves to every man's conſcience in the ſight of God.* It was the conſciouſneſs of this religious integrity,

integrity, or the teſtimony of conſcience to the power of it in his mind, that was the ground of his rejoicing. The word[a], which we render rejoicing, is elſewhere tranſlated, glorying; and the latter is its more literal meaning. I ſcarce need, however, to obſerve, that no other kind of glorying can be intended, than ſuch a juſt ſelf-approbation, as is the inſeparable attendant of habitual integrity, in a well-informed mind. This is intirely conſiſtent with a humble ſenſe of its imperfection, and obligations to the grace or free goodneſs of God, for all its attainments in knowledge and righteouſneſs; as the faculties, by which we acquire them, are his gifts, and all the means of improving theſe nobler powers of our nature are of his appointment, and the effects of his grace or favour. To him we are all highly indebted for his co-operating aids; though both Reaſon and Revelation teach us to regard them, as ever communicated

[a] καύχησις

in

in a way perfectly conſiſtent with the agency of man; not as ſuperſeding, but aſſiſting that moral culture, which is our indiſpenſible duty, and which immediately depends on our own proper choice. This humble and grateful ſenſe of our dependence on the Father of our ſpirits, for our attainments in goodneſs, in the view now given, while it is intirely conſiſtent with the juſt applauſes of an approving conſcience, is alſo in itſelf a very important branch of that religious temper, the conſciouſneſs of which is the foundation of our glorying or rejoicing. St. Paul was a moſt illuſtrious example of the influence of this truly pious and Chriſtian diſpoſition. Accordingly in the text, with that conſcious integrity, in which he rejoiced, he unites the important conſideration of the grace or favour of God, as aiding and animating him in the acquiſition of it.

I ſhall only juſt add here, that in the glorying or rejoicing, of which the apoſtle ſpeaks,

ſpeaks, we are undoubtedly to conſider him as including, both the preſent inward ſatisfaction, which he experienced, ariſing from the judgment of his own mind; and likewiſe the glorious hope of that immortal life and bleſſedneſs which the goſpel ſet before him; as a reward, which would amply compenſate all his labours and ſufferings, and crown his utmoſt wiſhes. That the character of the Apoſtle fully correſponded to the view of it given in the text, the hiſtory which we have of his life, in the writings of the New Teſtament, affords us the cleareſt and moſt ſatisfactory evidence.

But not to enter into this at preſent; I haſten to the proper application of the paſſage, which I ſhall

I. Conſider, as deſcriptive of the temper and conduct of the faithful miniſters of Chriſt in general. I ſhall then,

II. More particularly direct your thoughts to that bright example of ſuch a chaa character, which has been ſet before us in the life and converſation of our departed friend.

Theſe views of the ſubject will ſuggeſt ſome further reflections, conſolatory and inſtructive, as the improvement of the whole.

I. Of the declaration of St. Paul in the text, as applicable to the faithful miniſters of Chriſt in general.

It is deſcriptive, (1.) Of the integrity of their views and conduct in the exerciſe of their miniſtry. And (2.) Of the happy effect of it, in the ſatisfactions and joys, which flow from the teſtimony of conſcience to the prevailing influence of ſuch a principle.

(1.) As to the principle itſelf, by which they are governed in their public labours, or, agreeably to our Apoſtle's language, in the general tenor of their converſation with the world. Though the miniſters of the goſpel are not, in common, expoſed to the ſame difficulties and dangers as the apoſtles were; they are, however, by no means exempt from all trials of their integrity. If they are not under the like temptations to a total apoſtacy from the Chriſtian faith, they are yet not without their diſcouragements in a ſteady adherence to what, upon careful examination, appears to them to be the genuine truth of Chriſtianity.

Not to proceed too far into this copious ſubject—In the miniſtry among Proteſtant Diſſenters, though the liberty of private judgment is, among Chriſtians of that denomination, an acknowledged principle; and is, indeed, the only rational ground of their ſeparation from all religious eſtabliſhments; it is yet not to be denied, that they are far from being conſiſtent in maintaining the exercise of that principle in its proper extent. Many there are, who, while they claim this privilege for themſelves, will by no means allow the ſame liberty to others. Creeds and confeſſions, of meer human authority, which have no better an origin and ſupport than the opinion of fallible men (deſerving and venerable as their characters may be in ſome reſpects) are too commonly held in a degree of eſtimation, to which they can have no juſt claim: and though the ſanction of the civil power may be denied, as having, in truth and reaſon, any weight to enforce the reception of them; they are yet implicitly followed, with an equally blind ſubmiſſion, as any formularies whatever, which are magiſterially eſtabliſhed and defended. I am ſorry to add, few, comparatively, are thoſe diſſenting ſocieties, in which a true liberality of ſpirit ſo far generally obtains, as to admit their miniſters to think and judge freely for themſelves; or, at leaſt, to ſpeak, with freedom and without reſerve, what they apprehend to be the pure, uncorrupted doctrines of Revelation.

There are too often ſome favourite points of doctrine; at beſt, matters of dark and doubtful diſputation, if not doctrines notoriouſly repugnant to the dictates of reaſon and common ſenſe; or, which is much more to be regretted, doctrines, which, though, I doubt not, they are viewed in a very different light by many who hold them, do in themſelves directly tend to weaken the obligations, if not ſap the very foundation of morality, by furniſhing falſe grounds of hope, and ſuch as are independant on moral and perſonal righteouſneſs; there are, I ſay, ſome points of doctrine of this nature, which, abſurd as they are in themſelves and hurtful in their tendency, are too often looked upon, as attended with that certainty, and deemed ſo ſacred, that for a miniſter to be ſilent about them, but, ſtill more, to declare againſt them, is ſufficient to incur upon him the heavy charge of unſoundneſs in the faith, and render him odious to thoſe, whom he wiſhes to ſerve in their beſt intereſts.

I forbear

I forbear purſuing theſe unpleaſing, though too well-grounded reflections; and ſhall conclude them with obſerving, that theſe are circumſtances, which have a very diſcouraging aſpect on the miniſterial character, and are no inconſiderable trials of the integrity of many, who have taken it upon them. In ſuch a ſituation, what judicious Chriſtian will doubt the propriety of our adopting the noble ſentiment of St. Peter, as the rule of our conduct, namely, that *we ought to obey God, rather than men*[b]? Truth is the cauſe of God. Of this we profeſs ourſelves miniſters; and are, therefore, by the nature of our office, called upon to ſtand forth in its defence, and to endeavour to the utmoſt of our power to promote the knowledge of it.

All truths are not, indeed, of equal moment. Unqueſtionably, thoſe, which relate to practice, are of the higheſt importance, and ought chiefly to be inſiſted

[b] Acts v. 29.

on.

on. There is alſo a great diverſity both in the gifts, which the great Father and Lord of all hath ſeen fit to impart to thoſe who are engaged in the work of the miniſtry, and in the capacities and taſte of thoſe among whom they labour. This not only admits of, but calls for, ſome difference in the manner in which miniſters are reſpectively to conduct their miniſtrations; each taking care to make choice of that, by which they are likely to render themſelves moſt inſtrumental to the edification of their hearers. But ſtill all ſhould be conſiſtent with ſimplicity and godly ſincerity; which, if they form the heart, will have a governing influence on all the ſervices of thoſe, who preach the word. The faithful ſervant of Jeſus will honeſtly, and without diſguiſe, impart the reſult of his enquiries, on all thoſe grand points which concern the duty and happineſs of man. All duplicity of ſpeech he will carefully avoid; conſidering it as a practice no leſs diſhonourable in itſelf, than it is incompatible with the proper deſign of his office, by a ſervile accommodation to the prejudices of mankind, to ſtrengthen, inſtead of correcting, their miſtakes, and confirm them in error, inſtead of leading them into the knowledge of the truth. In a word, he will not ſhun to declare to them the whole counſel of God, reſpecting their everlaſting ſalvation; but, in conformity to the advice of our Apoſtle to Timothy, and Titus[c], he will *in meekneſs inſtruct thoſe that oppoſe themſelves; reprove, rebuke, exhort, with all long-ſuffering; in all things, ſhewing himſelf a pattern of good works, in doctrine uncorruptneſs, gravity, ſincerity, ſound ſpeech that cannot be condemned, that he that is of the contrary part may be aſhamed, having no evil to ſay of him.* And great muſt be the happineſs, which every miniſter of this deſcription enjoys in this world: for whatever difficulties or diſcouragements of an

[c] 2 Tim. ii. 25. Chap. iv. 2. Titus ii. 7, 8.

external nature he may meet with; he has a treaſure within him, which is of incomparably ſuperior worth to all the treaſures of earth, even that inward ſolid peace and ſatisfaction, which the world can neither give nor take away.

Of this happy effect of godly ſincerity, in the diſcharge of the miniſterial duty, I now proceed to ſpeak. Having before hinted at the extenſive influence of bigotry and uncharitableneſs, in matters of religious opinion; I ſhould be greatly wanting, did I not obſerve, on the other hand, that the cauſe of truth and liberty has a conſiderable, though, in a comparative view, but a ſmall, number of ſteady friends and generous ſupporters, by whoſe concurrence and liberality, miniſters of the ſame enlarged turn of mind are, in ſome degree, encouraged to go on in the proſecution of their ſtudies and labours.

But, at the ſame time, while narrow, party ſyſtems, and almoſt every ſpecies of doctrine which the ignorance or artifice of man can devise, and which are as unintelligible, as they are indefensible, aided by the efforts of a blind, but furious zeal, are daily increasing their votaries; how notorious and visible is the declension among the friends of free inquiry, and liberal sentiments! Hence neglect, and detraction, become the trying lot of many, whose time and talents are employed in promoting the noble cause of religion and virtue amongst mankind. Painful, however, as these returns are for their upright and diligent labours; their conscious integrity and hope of the divine approbation give a firmness and stability to their minds, which alleviates all their mortifications and trials. To secure the testimony of that inward witness, which is either the best friend or the worst enemy of man, is the ultimate view of every one, who worthily fills the ministerial character: and his heart not condemning him, he has confidence towards God. If his pious and benevolent endeavours have not been crowned with the ſucceſs he wiſhed; he has, yet, the ſatisfaction of reflecting, that he has been ſteady in his adherence to the great intereſts of truth and virtue, and has not baſely ſacrificed them, for the ſake of popular applauſe or ſordid gain. That ſublimeſt of all joy, which ſprings from this teſtimony of conſcience, renders him calm and ſubmiſſive under all the evils he ſuffers; adds a true reliſh to every bleſſing which he ſhares; and animated by its cheering influences, he anticipates the awful hour of his diſſolution with compoſure and reſignation; till, having finiſhed his courſe, and kept the faith, he is called to receive the glorious future reward of all his labours and ſufferings, even that crown of righteouſneſs, which the Lord hath promiſed to them, who love and obey him.

In the brief delineations now given, and in which I have endeavoured to ſet forth, in a general view, the ſpirit and deſign of the apoſtle's deſcription in the text; we have thoſe moral features, which are ſo truly characteriſtic of our departed friend, as muſt have pointed him out to the lively remembrance of all who knew him. So conſpicuous and exemplary was the integrity of the late Reverend Dr. Caleb Fleming, as to be almoſt univerſally acknowledged and admired, and even by thoſe who differed moſt from him in their religious ſentiments. They, who had any acquaintance with him, could not but obſerve that he ſtood eminently diſtinguiſhed by an honeſt plainneſs of heart, a diſintereſted regard to what appeared to him to be truth and right; inſomuch that there was ſcarcely any one, who was not ready to declare their full conviction, of the ſtricteſt conformity, in all his miniſtrations, to the dictates of his beſt judgment, and of the rectitude of the views upon which he acted; much as they might think him miſtaken in ſome of his opinions, and though they might enter-

tain

tain the moſt formidable apprehenſions of their tendency.—A teſtimony this, to the character of our friend, which does him the higheſt honour, and is much more to be valued, than the warmeſt eulogiums, which could have been beſtowed upon him, either for the clearneſs and rationality of the doctrines which he preached, on the one hand, or the ſuppoſed orthodoxy of them, on the other.

In thoſe well-known ſtrictures of our admired poet,

An honeſt man's the nobleſt work of God.
For modes of faith let graceleſs zealots fight,
His can't be wrong whoſe life is in the right.
ESSAY ON MAN, Ep. 4. l. 248. Ep. 3. 305, 306.

But your expectations, and my own deſires, lead me to be more particular[d].

He

[d] The Doctor, in his 70th year, drew up ſome memoirs of his life, which he left to his particular friend, and relation by marriage, the Reverend Mr. Joſeph Towers, to be diſpoſed of at his diſcretion.

He was born at Nottingham, of reputable parents, who had a very respectable descent. He very early discovered an uncommon taste for literature, and seems also, from his earliest youth, to have had an inclination to the ministerial character. A close attention was given by his parents to the culture of his mind; who, likewise, consulting his genius, put him under proper masters, to instruct him in classical, as well as other branches of learning; though their views do not appear to have been directed to that profession, of which he became so bright an ornament. So early, as between the years of six and seven, he had made a considerable degree of proficiency in the knowledge of the Latin language; to which, and other studies of the like nature, he continued his attention for several years after. At about sixteen years of

Accordingly, from those memoirs I am furnished with most of the incidents related in the following account.

age,

age, he applied himſelf to the ſtudy of Logic, Ethics, Natural Philoſophy, and Aſtronomy, in which he had the aſſiſtance of the Reverend Mr. John Hardy[e], a learned divine, and a man of a very liberal mind. He was alſo inſtructed in Geometry and Trigonometry, by a Mr. Needham, who was diſtinguiſhed for his ſkill in thoſe ſciences, and under his care, he went through ſeveral books of Euclid. He alſo had particular advantages for improvement in the knowledge of Theology from the inſtruction of the judicious and learned divine beforementioned, of which he made the beſt uſe; as he all along ſeems to have had his attention directed to that kind of knowledge, and to have made it his favourite purſuit. He continued at Nottingham for ſeveral years after, when he removed to London. Here

[e] Mr. Hardy lived in Nottingham, and, for many years, took the care of a ſmall number of pupils, who were boarded in his houſe, and inſtructed in various branches of literature.

he acquired a conſiderable intimacy with the Reverend Mr. John Holt, who was afterwards, for a number of years, one of the profeſſors of the Academy at Warrington. To that gentleman he alſo acknowledges himſelf greatly indebted, for aſſiſting and encouraging him in his ſtudies, and for much uſeful inſtruction. By his advice, he further improved himſelf in claſſical knowledge, and particularly applied himſelf to the ſtudy of the Greek and Hebrew languages; though he had not as yet come to any determination of taking upon him the miniſterial character.

From theſe anecdotes it appears, that a good foundation had been laying from early life, to qualify him for his after profeſſion; and though he did not enter upon it till long beyond the uſual time, yet few perſons have entered upon it better furniſhed, and eſpecially in that branch of knowledge, which is more peculiarly proper to this office, and neceſſary to the uſeful diſcharge of the duties of it. Such were his abilities and improvements, that, previous to his engaging in the miniſtry among the Proteſtant Diſſenters, he became noticed by the Reverend Dr. John Thomas, the preſent Biſhop of Wincheſter, by whom he was recommended to the regard of Sir George Fleming, the then Biſhop of Carliſle. In conſequence of this, the Biſhop ſent him a preſentation to a living in Cumberland, with the promiſe of a further ample proviſion. And here I cannot omit mentioning an inſtance of generoſity on the part of Dr. Thomas, which does no ſmall honour to his character. The benevolent-minded Prelate, apprehending our friend's circumſtances to be narrow, made him an offer of advancing a handſome ſum to defray the expences of a removal to ſo great a diſtance. This alluring encouragement was ſet before him at a time, when he had a wife and ſeveral children, having been early married to his now-mourning

widow,

widow, and was deſtitute of all reſources to provide for them, as he had then quitted the ſecular employment, in which for a number of years he was engaged. In this deſtitute condition, and with all the weight of a care upon him, in which every tender and affectionate feeling of his ſuſceptible heart muſt be deeply intereſted; diſapproving, on mature deliberation, the terms of conformity, with a fortitude, which marks out an uncommon elevation of mind, but, at the ſame time, with the juſt reſpect which was due to his compaſſionate and very obliging patrons, he declined accepting the propoſal. The part which that truly amiable woman, the ſympathetic companion of his life, and ſharer in his diſtreſſes, took in this matter, muſt not be overlooked. She kindly aided his pious and virtuous reſolution, by the fulleſt and tendereſt aſſurances of her chearful readineſs to undergo the moſt extreme hardſhips, rather than obtain relief at the expence of his integrity and peace.

peace. Such was the noble ſacrifice which this truly religious pair united in making to the calls of duty and conſcience; committing themſelves to the care of that merciful Providence, to whoſe ſacred will they gave this ſignal proof of the moſt cordial and unreſerved obedience. And from that Almighty Power and Goodneſs, in which they truſted, they ſoon derived that outward ſuccour in this time of their need, which has been matter of grateful remembrance to them ever ſince.

Having, not long after, began his miniſtry among the Diſſenters, and preached occaſionally, in different places in the country, and round the metropolis; he was, on the death of the Reverend Mr. Munckley, in the year 1738, choſen to ſucceed him, as paſtor of a congregation in Bortholomew Cloſe.

To that people he had a very honourable recommendation by Dr. Avery, who had been one of their miniſters. Soon after

after his election, he was ordained; which service he justly placed in the only rational point of view, of being recommended, by his fathers and brethren in the ministry, to the favour of God, and the affectionate regard of the people [f]. On this occasion, he asserted the freedom with which he thought, by consenting to no other confession, than a general declaration of his faith in the revelation of the Gospel; which, allow me just to observe here, as made before the people to whom we minister, stands upon a very different footing, from the making that, or any other declaration of our religious faith, at the requisition of the civil magistrate; and in compliance with his demand, as a condition of legal toleration. The ceremony of the imposition of hands he also refused

f The ministers, who assisted at his ordination were, Dr. Jeremiah Hunt, Mr. Samuel Chandler, Mr. Thomas Mole, Mr. George Benson, Mr. Joseph Symmonds, and Mr. Nathaniel Sandercock—Dr. Hunt preached, and Mr. Chandler gave the Charge.

to ſubmit to, becauſe he conſidered it as void of any juſt meaning, where no extraordinary gifts are, or can be, imparted.

In this ſituation he continued to officiate till the year 1753, when, on the declining health of that judicious, as well as eloquent, and, by all the friends of rational religion and free enquiry, greatly admired preacher, the Reverend Dr. James Foſter, then miniſter to a morning ſociety, at Pinners Hall, our friend was appointed to the office of Aſſiſtant-preacher to him, ſtill officiating in the afternoon at Bartholomew Cloſe. On the death of Dr. Foſter, which took place not long after, he was choſen to ſucceed the Doctor in the paſtoral office, in which view he had been alſo warmly recommended to the ſociety by his worthy and benevolent predeceſſor. It was not long after this appointment, before the Society in Bartholomew Cloſe, being greatly reduced, and that chiefly by the death of its aged members, was diſſolved, moſt of the remaining few uniting

them-

themſelves to the ſociety at Pinners Hall; where, as you well know, Dr. Fleming continued to officiate with a moſt exemplary aſſiduity, till diſabled by the growing infirmities of his far-advanced age, which did not lay him wholly aſide till within ſome months ſhort of two years before his death.

He began and ever purſued his miniſtry with a manly and truly Chriſtian liberality of mind; with-holding nothing that he thought profitable to his hearers, and opening to them his ſentiments on the ſeveral doctrines of religion with the greateſt freedom; to his views of which he fixed the attention of his audience, in an uncommon degree, by the eaſy and natural, but ſpirited and truly forcible, manner, in which his diſcourſes were delivered.

It might have been expected that ſo bright a manifeſtation of the influence of the true principle of religious liberty, the firſt and vital principle of the

the Proteſtant Diſſent, would particularly have recommended him to the affectionate eſteem of all the miniſters of that perſuaſion; but here I am ſorry to obſerve, from his own memoirs, the caſe was ſo much otherwiſe, that many of his brethren, and not only thoſe who were more Calviniſtic, but ſome who might well have been ſuppoſed to be better informed, inſtead of encouraging his labours, behaved towards him with great coolneſs and diſreſpect. This was as unfriendly as it was unmerited, and greatly tended to injure his reputation among the laity, and by that means to defeat his uſefulneſs, as well as expoſe him to difficulties. I will not further unveil this unpleaſing part of his hiſtory. Let the living be admoniſhed by it, to be more conſiſtent with themſelves, and act more worthy of the noble cauſe for which they profeſs themſelves advocates. Under the neglect and diſaffection of many, he had, however, the eſteem and countenance of a few others;

who, in their day and generation, were burning and ſhining lights, and who, being dead, yet ſpeak, in thoſe uſeful publications, which they have left behind them. I here particularly refer to thoſe learned and judicious divines, as well as pious and excellent men, the Reverend Dr. Jeremiah Hunt, and Dr. Nathaniel Lardner, the former of whom was the immediate predeceſſor of Dr. Foſter, at Pinners Hall. With both theſe miniſters he held a peculiar intimacy, and, as he reſpectfully and gratefully mentions, derived many advantages from it. Dr. Fleming, alſo, by his obliging temper and manners, by his improving converſation, but eſpecially and above all, by that freedom and fidelity, which appeared in his public miniſtrations, procured the higheſt regard from many reſpectable characters among the laity, whoſe generous ſupport he ſpeaks of with the utmoſt gratitude.

Our departed friend was an able and judicious defender of the truth of the

Goſpel-revelation, and a cloſe and diligent examiner of its ſacred content. He was a ſteady aſſertor of the rights of private judgment and conſcience, in their proper latitude and extent. He explained the Scriptures, as they appeared to him, with preciſion and freedom. The leading principles of that theory of religion which he taught, and which guided and animated all his miniſtrations, were ſuch as are highly honourable to God and friendly to man. Theſe, whatever there was of a critical or argumentative nature in his diſcourſes, he always took care to apply to their moral and practical uſes; enforcing all which he uttered in the pulpit, by the exemplary conſiſtency of his own temper and conduct. He had many proofs of the ſucceſs of his miniſtry; though he had alſo his difficulties and diſcouragements.

He diſtinguiſhed himſelf as an author as well as a miniſter. His publications were numerous; ſome on the moſt interefting fubjects, refpecting the common caufe of Chriftianity and liberty; and his difcuffions of thefe were fuch as were honoured with the approbation of not a few perfons of great judgment and learning, as well as high in rank and ftation.

Upon the whole, the life we have been furveying, was both a very honourable and ufeful one; our ideas of which would be ftill further heightened, were we to unite with his qualifications as a minifter, the many amiable virtues, perfonal and focial, which he exhibited in a private ftation. But to thofe who knew him, to fay more would be needlefs; and efpecially after the juft and pleafing delineation of his character, given, on the folemn occafion of his interment, by my Reverend friend and brother.

To apply the whole:

I. The fubject is in the higheft degree confolatory, under the lofs of fuch characters as we have been defcribing. To die—is, indeed, no other than an event to which we are are all liable at every age, and in all conditions of life. That the body, which is worn out by age, ſhould diſſolve and turn to duſt, is to be expected from the operation of thoſe laws, which the God of nature hath ordained, and is unavoidable. But ſtill a ſcene of death is in every inſtance awful; nor can the removal of thoſe, who have worthily filled the ſtations aſſigned them by Providence, ever take place, though deferred to the lateſt ſeaſon, without leaving impreſſions of ſerious concern on the thoughtful and well-inclined. The ſtroke muſt be yet more deeply felt, where the bonds of nature, or of friendſhip and love, have formed a cloſer and more endearing connection. We are not, however, left to ſorrow, as thoſe who are without hope. The goſpel adminiſters the beſt ſupport, by the full aſſurance, which it gives of a happy exchange of ſtates for the truly good, on departure hence. They rest from labours, and their works follow , to be crowned with that glorious ward, which the Lord hath promised to his faithful servants. To this source of strong consolation, let me point the attention of the friends of that venerable minister of Christ, who has now finished his work and obtained his dismission; to compose their spirits, and inspire submission to the merciful, though afflictive will of heaven. The sympathetic heart must feel in the tenderest manner for the affectionate widowed consort of this excellent man and best of husbands, who is mourning over the dissolution of the dearest of all connections, cemented by sixty years experience of the most perfect mutual amity. May the God of all comfort support her under this painful stroke, and the infirmities of her far advanced years!

2. The doctrine of the text, and the voice of Providence in the dispensation before

before us, afford matter of the moſt uſeful admonition.

Miniſters are hereby reminded of the indiſpenſible obligations they are under—to fidelity, in the communication of truth, according to their judgment and convictions.—to maintain a ſincere regard for promoting the influence of pure and undefiled religion, and the true, everlaſting happineſs of man—and to an upright diſcharge of all the duties of their office, with a humble dependance on the favour and bleſſing of the Almighty Father of Spirits, for the furtherance of thoſe important ends. It is this, and this alone, which will ſecure the teſtimony of conſcience, and lay a ſolid foundation for rejoicing both living and dying: while, if we are deſtitute of theſe beſt of all qualifications, in which-ever of the different denominations of Chriſtians we rank, or whatever opinions we may eſpouſe and defend; and whether we have been applauded or neglected by the

 world

world around us; in the hour of impartial reflection, our own hearts muſt reproach and condemn us, and we ſhall at laſt be numbered among the wicked and unprofitable.

They, who once enjoyed the benefit of our departed friend's miniſtrations, will allow me juſt to hint, how highly it concerns them, to remember him, who ſpake unto them the word of God, and to follow his faith, conſidering the end of his converſation.. They will permit me particularly to point to their recollection the ſtability of his adherence to the Chriſtian faith, not as laid down in any eſtabliſhed, or party ſyſtems, but as taught in the genuine records of the goſpel revelation. In the belief of that revelation, he was fully confirmed by the external evidence with which it came attended, and which he conſidered, as amounting to a clear and ſatisfactory proof of its divine original. It was from that pure fountain of truth, that he drew all his inſtructions, and on its gracious aſſurances and precious promiſes he built his hopes: nor was there any thing which he more reſented, than the idea of his joining iſſue with the infidel, becauſe he laboured to expoſe thoſe irrational doctrines, which were matter of offence to both. " So far (ſays the Doctor in his Memoirs) " we are agreed; but then my " deſign has had a contrary direction; " namely, to point out the rational in- " terpretation and its divine evidence. " Whereas the unbeliever has played off " all his ridicule at the abuſive repre- " ſentations of Chriſtianity, in order to " throw contempt on the very idea of a " divine revelation. We have agreed in " pulling down the abſurdity, but have " differed widely about eſtabliſhing the " reality." You, his friends, who highly eſteemed and honoured him, and who are fully apprized of the clearneſs and propriety of theſe his diſtinctions, will not forget his ſolid reaſonings, nor loſe the

con-

convictions which they wrought in your minds, but by reflection on the one, will give ſtrength and permanence to the other. With your faith you will alſo unite thoſe ſeveral virtues and graces of character, which he taught from the pulpit and enforced by his example in private; that you, like him, may, in the teſtimony of conſcience, enjoy that noble fruit of integrity, which time will improve, but accident can never blaſt.

Finally, The inſtruction of the apoſtle and the preſent call of Providence extend to us all. They powerfully exhort —to fidelity in our ſeveral ſtations, public or private—to that honeſty of principle and rectitude of conduct—that undiſſembled piety and inflexible virtue—that devotion of mind, in the performance of all the external duties of religion, and that juſt dealing in our worldly tranſactions: in a word, they loudly admoniſh us to cultivate that ſimplicity and godly ſincerity, which are the ſprings of true goodneſs, nefs, and the beft fecurity to the regular practice of it—which form the character of the upright man and the real Chriftian, and which will make us happy in ourfelves and ufeful to others—So fhall both minifters and people rejoice together here, and the teftimony of our confcience be finally confirmed and honoured with the plaudit of our merciful Lord and Mafter, the appointed judge of quick and dead, in that all-enlivening fentence, *Well done, good and faithful fervants, enter ye into the joy of your Lord*[g]; and God grant that this may be the honour and happinefs of us all. Amen.

[g] Matt. xxv. 23.

Lately published by the Author of the
SERMON.

I. PRAYERS for Families and Persons in Private. Price 3s. bound.

II. FREE THOUGTS on a Dissenter's Conformity to Religious Tests. Price 1s.

III. A DEFENCE of the LIBERTY of MAN as a Moral Agent: In Answer to Dr. Priestley's Illustrations of Philosophical Necessity. Price 3s. sewed.

Printed for J. Johnson, No. 72, St. Paul's Church-yard; and C. Dilly, in the Poultry.

AN

ORATION,

DELIVERED AT

THE INTERMENT,

JULY 29, 1779.

THE

FUNERAL ORATION.

THE most caſual ſurvey of thoſe numerous manſions of the dead, which this place exhibits to our view, muſt have a natural tendency to inſpire ſome degree of ſerioufneſs and recollection even into the moſt thoughtleſs and inattentive. The tombs around us proclaim, in the moſt emphatic terms, that *it is given unto all men once to die.* Nor can any be wholly inſenſible, that as theſe graves are filled with the remains of our fellow-creatures, ſome of them perhaps once our friends, it cannot be long before we alſo muſt deſcend into the ſame dreary habitations. The various ſcenes of life are, indeed, perpetually pointing out to us, that our reſidence here is only temporary. *As for man, his days are as graſs,*

as

as a flower of the field, so he flourisheth; the wind passeth over it, and it is gone, and the place thereof shall know it no more. Whatever may be the possessions, whatever the attainments of human beings, they must all in a few years quit this scene of action, and launch into the regions of futurity. This is the inevitable lot of all, of the poor and of the rich, of the weak and of the powerful, of the ignorant and of the learned. No age, no sex, no rank or dignity, is exempted from the general decree. Whoever thou art, whatever thy situation, thy character, or thy circumstances, *Dust thou art, and unto dust thou shalt return.*

We are now assembled to commit to the silent grave, the body of our late reverend, and departed friend and brother, Dr. CALEB FLEMING, who sustained, for many years, with much reputation, the character of a Protestant Dissenting Minister in this metropolis. He hath finished his labours, and is gone to make up his account with his great Maſter, with his and our common Lord. Indefatigable in the purſuit of truth, and zealous in the promotion of what he apprehended to be ſo, he ſpent the greater part of a long life in the duties of the miniſterial office. A very large portion of his time, for a conſiderable ſeries of years, was entirely appropriated to the ſtudy of divinity, and to thoſe parts of knowledge which are immediately connected with it; other ſtudies engaged comparatively little of *his* attention; theology was at once his buſineſs and his pleaſure. Ordinary amuſements and modes of relaxation were little adapted to his taſte. For though he had naturally great chearfulneſs of temper, yet the gravity of the Divine eminently predominated in his character. Of the rights of conſcience he was a warm and reſolute aſſertor; and ever oppoſed, with a manly indignation, all invaſions of the right of private judgment. He was a Proteſtant, and a Protestant Dissenter, from inquiry, and upon principle. He engaged in the pursuit of truth with perseverance, and with ardour; and those who differed from him in opinion could not question his sincerity, if they were under the influence of candour, or of equity. He had refused liberal offers to enter into the establishment, and such as, in the circumstances he then was, he must have accepted, had he been influenced by lucrative views. But his integrity was unquestionable; and he delivered his opinions in the pulpit, with so much seriousness and energy, and such a degree of openness and frankness, as naturally impressed his auditors with a strong conviction of his sincerity. He paid no regard to established systems, and considered the interposition of human power and authority in matters of religion, as the principal source of the corruptions in Christianity. This sentiment, which is certainly well grounded, he was extremely solicitous to inculcate, both in his preaching, and in his writings. His ſeriouſneſs and piety, the uprightneſs of his character and conduct, the abilities which he diſplayed as a preacher, and his many private and ſocial virtues, procured him many reſpectable friends, and entitled him to general eſteem. Towards the cloſe of his life, he was rendered incapable of the public exerciſe of his miniſtry, by bodily weakneſs and diſeaſe. But even then a remarkable chearfulneſs and vivacity were often obſervable in him, till the powers of nature became nearly exhauſted, and his enfeebled frame announced his approaching diſſolution. As a man, he was an object of much regard and eſteem; and as a divine, and a diligent inquirer after religious truth, let his numerous publications ſpeak for him.

But the true deſign of funeral addreſſes of this kind, is, not chiefly to do honour to the dead, but to benefit the living; to awaken a ſenſe of that common mortality, to which we are all ſubject; and which, neverthelefs, human beings are too apt to forget. The fhortnefs of human life, though it is one of thofe obvious truths of which none can be ignorant, is yet too feldom practically remembered. The generality live as if this were to be the whole of their exiftence: they are anxious to procure the advantages, the conveniencies, and the enjoyments of the prefent life; but they make little provifion for futurity.

Far different fhould be the conduct of Chriftians; and far different will be their conduct, if the principles of the religion they profefs have their proper effect. They fhould live by faith: an habitual perfuafion of the reality and importance of the great truths of the Gofpel fhould influence their whole conduct. If fentiments like thefe have made a deep and juft impreffion on our hearts, terreftrial objects will appear comparatively of little importance. What was it that led the earlier profeffors of Chriftianity to undergo every ſuffering, every preſſure of diſtreſs, every calamity that human power could bring upon them, with patience, with ſerenity, with the moſt heroic fortitude? It was that faith in the great truths of religion, in the infinitely-momentous doctrines of the Goſpel, which made them conſider all temporary ſufferings as trivial, compared with the future and immortal bleſſedneſs which Chriſt had ſet before them. They had *reſpect unto the recompenſe of reward.* They were animated by the proſpects which the author and finiſher of our faith had ſet before them. We profeſs the ſame religion, and ſhould be influenced by the ſame principles; and if this be in reality the caſe, it will be productive in us of a ſimilar conduct. We ſhall then think nothing of ſo much importance to us, as to obtain the favour and approbation of our great Judge. We ſhall then look not chiefly *at thoſe things which are ſeen, and which are temporal; but at the things which are not ſeen, and which are eternal.*

One of the moſt mournful ſcenes in human life, is that of taking our laſt farewell of thoſe whom we have long loved and eſteemed, and who are about to deſcend into the grave. But this ſeparation would be rendered much more painful, were it not for the proſpects which religion ſets before us. This is our great conſolation, when we are deprived of our virtuous and pious friends by death, that on their departure from this world, the righteous are removed to *mount Zion, to the city of the living God, to the heavenly Jeruſalem; to an innumerable company of angels, to the general aſſembly and church of the firſt-born, to God the judge of all, to the ſpirits of juſt men made perfect, and to Jeſus, the mediator of the New Covenant.* Sentiments and views like theſe will naturally alleviate the diſtreſsful reflexions which may ariſe in the breaſts of the ſurviving relatives of our late honoured and departed friend, in conſequence of the loſs which by his death they have ſuſtained.

Death

Death puts an end to all our temporal cares, to all our temporal purſuits, to all our temporal enjoyments: but it puts not an end to our being. We quit this ſcene; but we are removed to another infinitely more important. What will be our ſituation there, is an inquiry of all others the moſt intereſting. Can there be one around me indifferent, what will be his future allotment, what the ſentence which he ſhall receive at the bar of the Almighty? It is impoſſible. Nothing but groſs and ſhameful inattention to the great truths of religion, can conceal from us their importance.

When we leave theſe manſions of the dead, let not thoſe ſalutary impreſſions be wholly loſt, which may on this occaſion have been excited. As we know, that we are mortal; as we know, that a few years will put a period to our temporal exiſtence; let us improve the time with which we may yet be favoured by the all-gracious Author of our being; let us cul-

tivate

tivate all the virtues which ſhould adorn the Chriſtian character, and by which our divine Maſter himſelf was ſo illuſtriouſly diſtinguiſhed. At the laſt day, when the trumpet of the archangel ſhall ſound, when all who are in their graves ſhall hear the voice of the Son of God, it will then be of infinite importance to us, what part, what character we ſhall have ſuſtained, what ſhall have been the general tenor of our conduct, in the preſent world. It will then be of infinite importance to us, whether we ſhall be numbered among the righteous or the wicked; among thoſe who have ſerved God, or thoſe who have ſerved him not. Let us then fix our views upon the end of life; and be induced, by the certainty of its approach, ſincerely and diligently to keep the commandments of God. Then may we rejoice in hope, that *this corruptible body ſhall put on incorruption*, and that *this mortal ſhall put on immortality*. Amen.

The

The following is a Liſt of most of the Pieces publiſhed by the late Reverend CALEB FLEMING, D. D.

I. AN Eſſay on Public Worſhip — 1729

II. An Anſwer to the Diſpute Adjuſted, 1732

III. The Jeſuit Unmaſked — 1735

IV. The Fourth Commandment abrogated by the Goſpel — — 1736

V. A Plain Account of the Law of the Sabbath — — — 1736

VI. A Letter to Dr. Cobden — 1738

VII. Remarks on Mr. Thomas Chubb's Diſſertation on Providence —— 1738

VIII. Remarks on his Vindication of the True Goſpel —— —— 1739

IX. Delays dangerous about the Repeal of the Teſt-Act — — 1739

X. Animadverſions on T. Chubb's Diſcourſe on Miracles —— 1741

XI. Plea for Infants — — 1742

XII. The Pædo-baptiſt defended againſt Mr. Burroughs —— 1745

XIII. A Ma-

XIII. A Manual for common Chriſtians 1750

XIV. A Catholic Epiſtle — 1744

XV. An Eſſay on Redemption 1745

XVI. An earneſt Addreſs to Britons 1745

XVII. The Immorality of profane Swearing 1746

XVIII. Truth and modern Deiſm at Variance 1746

XIX. A modern Plan — 1748

XX. A Comment on Warburton's Alliance 1748

XXI. St Paul's Heretic — 1748

XXII. True Deiſm the Baſis of Chriſtianity 1749

XXIII. A Letter to the Lay-Expoſitor 1749

XXIV. The Character of Thomas Bradbury, taken from his own Pen 1749

XXV. The Oeconomy of the Sexes 1751

XXVI. An Apology for Lord Bolingbroke 1752

XXVII. Theophilus to Gaius — 1753

XXVIII. A Sermon on the Death of the Rev. Dr. James Foſter — 1753

XXIX. An Apology for a Proteſtant Diſſent, 1755

XXX. Three Letters on Syſtematic Taſte 1755

XXXI. A Scale

XXXI. A Scale of First Principles 1755

XXXII. A Letter to Mr. Pyke 1756

XXXIII. A Letter to Mr. John Wesley 1756

XXXIV. Three Questions resolved 1757

XXXV. Necessity not the Origin of Evil, against Mr. Soame Jenyns 1757

XXXVI. A Survey of the Search after Souls 1758

XXXVII. A Defence of the Survey 1759

XXXVIII. A Sermon on St. Paul's Othodoxy 1759

XXXIX. The Nature, Design, and End of Christ's Death —— 1760

XL. The Equality of Christians in the Province of Religion 1760

XLI. The Merits of Christ exemplary 1761

XLII. The Palladium of Great Britain and Ireland —— 1762

XLIII. The Doctrine of the Eucharist 1763

XLIV. Christ's Temptation in the Wilderness —— —— 1764

XLV. The Claims of the Church of England seriously considered 1764

XLVI. An Antidote for the Rising Age 1765

XLVII. The Friendship and Virtue of David and Jonathan —— 1765

XLVIII. Ano-

XLVIII. Another Defence of the Unity 1766
XLIX. The Root of Proteſtant Errors examined —— 1767
L. Civil Eſtabliſhments in Religion a a Ground of Infidelity 1767
LI. A Letter from a Proteſtant Diſſenting Miniſter to the Clergy of the Church of England —— 1768
LII. A Supplement to Dr. Chauncy's Letter to Mr. T. B. Chandler 1768
LIII. The Open Addreſs of New Teſtament Evidence, or three plain Monuments, &c. —— 1771
LIV. Free Thoughts on a Free Enquiry into the Authenticity of the two firſt Chapters of St. Matthew's Goſpel —— 1771
LV. Diſcourſes on the three eſſential Principles of the Goſpel Revelation, which demonſtrate its divine Original —— 1772
LVI. Religion not the Magiſtrate's Province —— 1773
LVII. A Diſſertation on Self-murder 1773
LVIII. The Ingratitude of Infidelity 1775

F I N I S.

www.ingramcontent.com/pod-product-compliance
Lightning Source LLC
Chambersburg PA
CBHW021526090426
42739CB00007B/798